I Might Imagine Wild Things

A book of poetry

Sheena Stimpfl

First Edition, Paperback. October 2025. United States.

ISBN: 978-1-957863-50-4

Editing/Proofreading by Sheena Stimpfl

https://sheenastimpfl.substack.com/

For Norah and Theo

A Balance of Things

In the budding morning hours
Ripe with stillness and the rare quiet
I feel my aloneness

It is not unwelcome
But full of deep expansion and breath
Quiet thoughts to ruminate in

The anticipation of little feet shuffling
Movement making its way into the light
That begins trickling in

These moments are to be savored

The quiet
With the unrest
A balance never gaining its footing

I will want the noise
The chaos
I will long for it

There is value in the turbulence
But my god
It is so fleeting
And I swear
I can hear my heart breaking

The quiet becomes a loud roar
And it could feel like madness

Sway

Would it be easier
To understand
The complexity of emotions
Their constant sway
Of back and forth
Cold to warm
As the way that it is
And let it be that

A ride home
After a long day
And the winter's sun
Has all but disappeared

The falling snow from earlier
So beautiful the moment it fell
Has left a cold dampness
In its exit

There is a gloom
That rests in my bones
Some element that's missing

And in a moment
Of complete unexpectancy
A cluster of birds lift off
Just ahead
And their dance
Of undulation and synchronicity
Can even move mountains

And how could you not smile
In such moments of grace
Such a gift for the eyes
To feast on
For the soul to feel something
A bit warmer

How many moments
Of such beauty
Have gone by
Unseen

Today I did see
And maybe tomorrow, again
A shift made in moments
Immeasurable, mostly

I'll walk a little taller
And maybe float
By the end of the week

North Shore Drive

We took tea on the dock
The evening before
We were never too far from home
But we could've been anywhere

After that first sun
We sat under the awning in the slow rain
And we watched the heron
Make her graceful climb through the elements
A messenger of the gods
Navigating between life and death

You grasped nature with your bare hands
And you ground it down
And we set sail
We're going too slow! I declared
(Too prematurely and not for my own good)

You rocketed us into hysterics
And we made such bold statements
So serious and all too silly
I never laughed so hard with you

I believe that

You found me curled in on myself
Under the luxurious duvet and the pillows I coveted
My mind played a million reels
And it showed me such depths
I used to ignore

This will all make sense one day, it whispered

And I believed that, too

You sat on the patio
And watched from across the lake
As your father lounged in a chair
But he's been long gone now

And I hear what you've been saying
All of these years
The dreams you have
The pressure to live up
To be such a man
How he appears in moments like this
And haunts you

Who's to say he doesn't exist everywhere
Anywhere
Never really too far from home

I Had

There is a dull ache
For the things I used to love
And have
And want

That ache doesn't tell me
If there's love lost for good
Or if it's nestled deep down
Just waiting for a nostalgic bump
For it to resurface
To shine its face to the sun

I had and I wanted
And sometimes that's not enough

There is no going back there
And even if I could
Would it be the same

My heart tells me no
But my head
Oh, my head
It tells me anything is possible

And would I betray myself
For just a glimpse
A feel
If only for a small time

I can tell you

That I won't

It's risky business
To just throw it all to the fire

I had and I wanted
And sometimes that just has to be enough

Good Faith

I listen in
As if the red maples
Carry all of the secrets
And the dirt beneath my feet
Could lead the way

Maybe the purple finch
Would fly ahead
And warn me of any uncertainty

If I cannot muster the strength
Gather myself in my hands
And offer up the truth
Then what is left
But to go back
And start over

And who cares anyway

There is sincerity
For the honest and bold
Perhaps even the audacious

The Inevitability of These Things

We worry over
If there is a god or a heaven
Something to be held in
When this body inevitably fails

But have you seen
The first snowfall of the season
The waves crashing along the shore line
Have you heard the mourning doves
Or the way the wind whistles through the trees
Have you heard the first intake of a baby's breath
And the cacophony of your heart
When your love enters the room

We needn't worry so hard
Over things that come on their own time
The inevitability of these things
Heaven or God

Take a walk amongst the trees
Or the stars

You just need to look up
Look in
They've been here all along

The Thief

I landed in the middle of my life
And I wondered where epic grief hovered
If she was sneaking around the corner
Always in wait
The fear of her pouncing
Just when everything felt right and good

Grief knows my name
She comes in waves
And small bursts

She sneaks in
Ever so gently

And I have asked grief many times
Why she takes it easy on me

Oh I have grieved, you see
I have grieved all the things
In my time
And yet she has not dealt a blow

And so I wait for her
To take something
Or someone
Perhaps me

She wakes me in the night
Peeking around the corner
And I silently plead to her

Not yet, please
I have too much to lose

When grief comes
For the last time
She will be merciless
I know

And so I wait

Esta

We used to find each other's eyes
Never a word
Need be spoken

I knew we'd grow
To understand one another
That this was not ok

Something had to be done

And so we left
In our own ways and times
You first
And I followed, of course
I always did

I felt you pull away
In so many ways
And I knew it meant something to you
So I understood
And I paved a way for your absence

I'd sleep on your mattress
Happy to take the floor
When you'd come home
And I'd hear your breathing in the night

It was the only sleep
That felt purely restful in those times

You moved
And I jumped
A shadow so constant
But you never seemed to mind

I'd walk your every move

Your husband became my brother
Your children, very much my own
In so many ways

And I cherished every moment
Every memory

But you moved further
And I could not jump so far
You took a piece of me that day
And I wandered alone
Forced to figure it out on my own
Finally
And all for the better

Who would I be now
If only made to be your shadow

You came home
As we always do
And I fell right back
Into pace with you
Never missing a beat

We have spent so much time

So many nights
Spilling our secrets
Telling our fears
And yet there is still so much
I do not know of you

Much like the air of your sign
There is no way to capture you

I see the fascination alight in others
The way your past lovers
Have all come undone

It's the way you move
Through the world
So detached and rebellious

Do they know how much you actually care
How your heart feels broken
Much of the time
Burdened by thoughts unspoken
And time lost
The things you have loved
That have laid broken in your hands

I do
I always have

An Extravagant Walk

I could not resolve between wrong or right
Safe or perilous
But my feet moved me forward, anyhow
The man on his bike stopped a bit ahead
Adjusting his seat
And I thought
Is this a ruse, something to fool me

And it scared me

I continued on
Despite myself
A path led further into the woods and I dare not go
On the other side of the trees
Cars drove on
Would they hear me scream

I realized after some time
At some point
I had stopped following my feet
And I let my head lead the way
In fear and anticipation
Of something that may or may not come

I could not be present with the sky and the trees
I could not hear the birdsong

And it saddened me

I say I will not live in fear

But we both know that can't be true
Not in the world, today
This world that seems to move backwards
The one that says I will not let you
The one that says you are less than

And it angers me

And so in what ways can I then honor myself
If I cannot freely walk in nature
Without pinning my ears

Where will you have me go
What will you have me do

I'll Take My Chances

In the early morning hours
I struggled in my motherhood
The lack
And the overwhelming newness
Of it all

The constant needing of things
Not so much for myself
Was a heavy weight to bear

My anger soared
To heights I had never known
And I beat my fists
My body intuitively knowing
To move
Many years before I learned
The deep wisdom
Of such things

I wavered and steadied
At alarming rates
And I did not recognize
The face that stared back
In the mirror
Most days

I felt I had channeled
The matriarch of my life
A thought so desperate
And unnerving

The times she cursed me
With such hatred and disdain

I learned then
That you can love someone
And hate them all the same

And how I berated myself
Such similarities
I could not bear
My anger undulating
In nights of little sleep
And desperate cries of needing

I could not find my own hands
Even in the light of day

There is always a choice
A turn in the road
Begging the question
Will you stay here
Or go into the unknown

Surely, not as scary
As the boiling blood
That coursed through my veins
Night after night

Motherhood reminded me
Of so much I had lost
And so much that had never been given

And when I was good and empty
I picked myself back up
And moved forward
Leaving the pain in the past
To damage no further

I could deal a replica of hands
And be no better
But I chose to turn
Taking my chances
In all terrains
Rough and smooth

A Fable

There really are no simple words
For such complexity

You are my blind spot
Where I would like to see

There really is nothing there at all
A tale woven in my mind
A dissociation
Not of reality
You know nothing of my aliveness

There really is not an ounce of truth
You are a fable

And as much as I've painted myself
The damsel in distress
I am the wicked witch in the tower
And you are so wise to be free of me

Open Season

I found you singing
Somewhere in the depths of winter
Always such sweet, sad melodies

There's a sort of power
In digging down
Giving the people what they want
Over and over
Even if it kills you

We want to know
That others are hurting
That there is some shared despair
A comfort in desperation
And equal measure of darkness
That gives permission of expression

Each combine moves on
No more than a backward glance
And you are still there
Amongst the sugar maples
Bearing the coldest of seasons

I bet I'd still find you singing
Come spring
The melodies still sad
But sweeter amongst the wood violets
Your resilience intact
If only hanging on by a thread

When you cry amongst your people
And they cheer for your pain
If only as a skewed means of solidarity
Does it pain you to know
That they walk away unscathed
Back to their lives and their loves
Leaving you to stand alone
Betting and hoping
That winter will find you
Perpetually digging deeper
Still

The Weight

There is a fine balance
In the weight of a feeling
And the risk
Of becoming too serious
In this life

The things I concern myself with

It's not enough
To be so sensitive
To things
But do you not feel the war

There is much to be feared
And a whole world
Of heaviness that seeps in
Occasionally

It is a mockery
This illusion of safety

Who says you can have it all

If we're to exit this place
The when and the how
Such a depth of mystery
Then maybe
I'll parade my fears
And spill out my vulnerability
For all to see

There's safety in letting go
And free falling

At least I knew
Where I stood

Free and Natural Things

The faces I pass
So pinched and serious

Did you not see
The way the sun peeked through the clouds
Just now
The birds that are serenading
Their audience, so oblivious

There is air to breathe
And trails to be walked
Where things are to be discovered

Could I transfer my enthusiasm
For just a moment
And convince you to try
And see
That there are spaces and places
So simple, at a glance
But so miraculous
If given the time

Have you seen an orchid
A peacock strolling
A swift breeze
Nudging the leaves
And the moments of wonder
Before the soft, sweet landing

If you have eyes

Please do not misuse them
They were made
To take in such beauty
So free to us all

Aether

I searched for you
In all of the places
I remembered you loved
And I did not find you there

But I heard your screams
On the ferris wheel
Your laughter in the theater
And your footfalls
Against the pavement

All echoes
Still dancing in the air

Someday I'll leave too
And the memories
Of all the noises you left here
Could all but disappear

But maybe that's what
Imagination and inspiration are
A random body
Walks through a cloud
Of all the goodness you left behind

And suddenly

You are a song
A book
A piece of art

To be consumed
Leaving the eyes
And the ears
And the mouths
Of perfect strangers
Full of you

You or Me

There is another life
That keeps me from sleep
Another person
I've molded to fit what suits me

These scenarios played out
To appease my boredom

And it was never a problem
Until it began keeping me awake
And sneaking into my lucid moments
Stealing presence from the people in front me of
And attempts of connection

I recognize this space
This place she has lived her whole life
It robbed me of her
As she danced with the illusions in her head

And I tell myself
It's not that bad
It could be worse
My handle is much stronger
And I know my limits

Her sensationalism moved her
Around and around
Further and further away
Until she did not recognize
Any kind of connection

We may have made

I tell myself
I am not her
But we both know
The parts that exist

Your stars collided with mine

You are in my bones
In every beat of my heart

And when they rear their ugly heads
Am I to blame her
Or myself

Perfect Form

I have bent
And twisted myself
Into shapes
Never made for me

And I begged the stars
And the moon
And the entire night sky
To cast me
Into something that fit

The universe responded
In kind at times
But mostly in lessons
And speeches
I refused to hear

I could not see
Beyond entire galaxies
And I compromised myself
In space and time

And all the while
I was there in perfect form
Ever changing
Never knowing
What was meant for me
Need not be sought

It had never left

Little Girl

One day she'll stop asking
For your help
She'll stop needing it

She'll start doing it on her own

She'll shut the door
Asking for privacy

And you'll stop going upstairs

The goodnights will turn
To echoed shouts
That may or may not be heard
Throughout the house

And one day
Her room will be empty

And she will only call
(Sometimes)
To say goodnight

A Legacy

I'll course correct
Count my breath
Choose the opposite
And run far away
From your rule of thumb

There will be no more yelling
No being left with people
Who are not to be trusted
No going hungry

The lights will stay on
For as long as we please
And the heat at a comfortable setting

There will be no hitting
No marks left to be hidden

There will be no escaping
For yet another bump
Or consuming of poison
So thick and blinding
That the children are left
To be forgotten

The floors will be clean
And the towels freshly laundered
The filth of so many years
Scraped away
Like we did to the walls of the bath

There will be no denial
Of abuse and neglect
Because it doesn't exist here
At all

And this will be my legacy
A different kind of life
Of love
Something so rich and pure
You would never even recognize it

Ignorance of Youth

We spent our youth
Sleeping under the stars on Jackson
Exploring every inch of the city
Before dawn

Our long walks to the pool
Barefoot, along twenty-two
Our backyard, the cemetery on seventh
A shortcut to the creek
Where we laid waste
To chasing boys and smoking cigarettes

The summer before I turned twelve
It wasn't the pre-teen changes
That shifted who we were
Only death could alter you like that

How close we came to such violence that day
Our intuition the only source we could thank
The peril we'd manage to find
Had such an appeal to our young, loose minds

But we hadn't need to search far
For the chaos and the dysfunction
That lay so easily in our own beds

She worked nights
A display of her body
For money that he rolled expertly
For the white horse

And we noticed
The way the boys stared
But mostly
The way the older ones lingered
And the uncles that asked for more than one kiss
Hugging just a little too long

And the trust placed so easily
In the sitters that never sat
And abused more than just their roles
The confusion of touch and love
Altered even more by the curiosity
Played out between two friends

And when twelve finally came
Only one of us ventured out
Seeking those boys that suddenly were very real

I'd numb myself in the grass
Mourning our childhood
Vanishing right before my eyes

Anxiety introduced itself to me
When we met in the seventh month
And I knew before the ninth month came
That our friendship was long gone
With our innocence

So I left for the mountains on Montana Road
And had hope for Harmony
Where I found solace and books
And walks through the countryside

That would shape my heart
While simultaneously breaking it

I found there is such a thing
As too much time alone

And I made new friends
But there was so much missing
Along with the hot water, heat, and food

I grew tired of the mistakes of others
Altering my very existence
Without me getting a say in the matter
Of the damp cold of this place we called home
Permeating my bones
Of a hunger never satiated
By the meager pantry offerings
Of reaching and calling out
And coming up empty

I cannot recall a time
Where there was peace
And warmth and hope
Always so fleeting
Right on the edge of depletion
Borrowed against a future time
That was never promised

To struggle and fear
Was commonplace
And I'd find myself on the roof
Night after night

Gazing out over the junkyard of our lives
With no clear vision
No hope of a bright future

And I yearned for the ignorance of youth
That I never actually had
Always so aware of my surroundings
And what felt so wrong

I did not find what was right
And real and warm
For so many years

And when I travel back
To those times and places
My stomach turns
But I know they shaped me
For better or worse

I just hope for the better

A Heavy Proposition

These old frustrating patterns
Of lessons already learned
Ebbing and flowing
Showing face

The most inconvenient
But really
The most fruitful
If you have the time

Darkness can bring such depths
And despair of the soul

But there is a curiosity of possibilities
There is a duality of life
The light and the dark
The masculine and the feminine

And who's to say which is worse
Each with gifts of their own to spare

I have held the light and the dark
Which is heavier
Depends on the day
You can see they're of equal measure
There cannot be one without the other

So fling yourself into nature
Into a quiet meditation
Of twisted poses

Escape to the mountains
And speak with the birds
Or the gods

Just do yourself a favor
And make the time
And come back and tell me
Of all the wonders your beautiful mind
Whispered in those spaces
You reasoned were too heavy

Turbulent Sea

Does anyone ever actually feel this much
I wonder
Quite often enough
That I believe it to be true

That at times I could burst
With the expansion of joy
Or disintegrate
With the crumbling of sorrow
So heavy and earth shattering

What could possibly cause such sadness

But surely the joy
Overrides such feelings
Each moment, a chance
An opportunity to find
A crumb of possibility
For something, anything
To feel good

I speak of the birds
In all of their synchromatic grace
Taking flight
And the wonder of such a sight
The tiny miracles of nature
And the flow of connection

There is an energy
So unspoken and right

And true
A blink and you miss it kind of feeling

But really, you can't
It never truly recedes
Even as we ignore it
And pay it no mind

But I am one of those
Cursed, at times it seems
To see it all
And feel so deeply
The crashing of the waves

The Gift

I'll paint a picture for you
Of my body
That you can take with you

A head of long, blonde waves
That bear the brunt of my boredom
And frustration
Never really safe
From a bout of hormones
Threatening to doubt an image
Taken so long to grow

Eyes that glow green
In mourning
When tears have taken over
Flooding their sight

My father's nose
A strong chin set on a square face
Attached to a sharp jaw
My mother's, no doubt

And these squared off shoulders
That could get too broad
With too much strength

Breasts that have given
And sustained life for years
But they've served their purpose now

And these strong arms
Made of carrying small bodies
Of rocking and holding

Hands so delicately showing signs of age
With their spots and veins
A thing of wonder
That takes my attention
And at times, my breath

A belly that never snapped back
In its elasticity
A hint of muscle underneath
With proof of three lives made within
Only two making it out

And these hips
Square and strong enough
For carrying them through

These legs I have hidden
The ones that never tan in the summer
The battle scars of veins
That had buckled under the weight
Of carrying lives

And these two feet
That carry me
Day after day
The long, thick scar shining brightly
For all to see

I look at my body
My forty year old body
And I do not recognize
Most of what I see

The outward changes do not mirror
My internal world

Not one bit

Inside I grow closer to childhood
To freedom
I grow younger by the year

But this body
Grows older by the day

I'll let it age
Gracefully
And I do not disparage it

It has given
And continues to give so much

Desolate

When loneliness surfaces
It makes no effort at all
To announce its presence

Coming on quickly
Pulsing and contracting
Birthing such sorrow
In its wake

There is no timeline
For its stay
As it ebbs and flows
Reaching out
And touching every surface
Making marks
On everything that once was clean
Now muddied and ruined

And when the desolate
Decides its fed enough
It endeavors to depart
Leaving crumbs
At times
Not worth gathering

Counterpart

If there is a memory
Of such goodness
From our past
I struggle to find it

And what should it matter, anyway
It's all good as gone
Dead and buried

Yet I search it out

There must be meaning
In there somewhere
A key to uncover
That will unlock
All of the struggles
And the patterns
I find so hard to break

There is a deeper, darker side
Way down
And I know it's you

I used to push her away
A disgrace
Something to be shamed for

And I'd turn my head
In the spaces
Where I'd sink down deep

And meet you there

I cursed and I swore
(This is not me)

But if she is a part of me
Isn't there something to be nurtured
Surely, it exists within me

And how I'd wish it away
Pray for it to rot and fester
Never knowing
That I, too
Would sink down
Attached at her heels

And so I have no choice
But to love her
To love you
Still hanging on, somehow
Regardless of any cords
Being cut
You are in my blood

To hate you
Is to hate myself
And unlike you
I won't do that

To punish myself so eagerly
When all we both ever really wanted
Was to be loved

Old Friend

There are so many people
Bumping into one another
Half-hearted
No apologies offered up

And the breathing space
Feels all but taken
But no one's really breathing here

The parking spaces are limited
Classes are full
Lines are long
And no one is really looking up
Are they

I don't recognize anyone around me
And they, too
Wouldn't know my name
Even though I've told them
Many times

If connection is currency
Than we are sufficiently suffering
And lost
And poor

I don't know about you
But I've decided to go to the woods, anyhow
If I am to be alone
And misunderstood

Then I'll find my old friend
In the sun rays
That offer such warmth and knowing

So much so
I understand
I was never really alone

All I Can See

I sat in one spot
And I watched from the window
As the wind shook the bare trees
And the sunlight spilled in
Through the front windows
Happily and lazily
Landing on the floor

Everything seemed normal

Time passed second by second
But all I could see
Was the growth of my children
The changes in our home over time
The season outside
So violent and offending

And it'll change
As all of these things do
Time and again
And we'll say things like

Where does the time go
They grew right before our eyes

But it's moments like these
When I can sit
In my one spot
And I can watch it
With wide open eyes

I can see the change happen
Right before me

The growth
The dimming of the light
As the sun sinks low

It doesn't go anywhere

These changes
You can observe
Pure movement
In such stillness

If that's your thing

The Head

There is a war
A constant fury of sorts
Two sides to every coin

There is a reason
The head is above the heart

A constant push and pull
One or the other
Who knows which is right
The other
Never nearly wrong
Just not loud enough
I suppose

If the heart beats
Hard enough
To throw our bodies
Into submission
Then the head screams
Loud enough
A thunder pulsing
It drowns the whole world

There are noises so bright
They blind
Even if dialogue
Is spoken within normal range

It is this place

That only knows silence
And stillness
With measured practice
A constant belt of sounds
Of clamor and racket
A dissonance
Of what's inside
Compared to what's out

I suppose the heart
Could be the same

A decision of senses
What to feel
Or what to hear
Because I cannot do both

The Heart

How else should I wear
My heart
If not on my sleeve
Or walking around
Outside of my body

The heart
Finds its way out
Into the world
Placed in another's hands
Or put into your work

If it's not bursting
Or lost
Or crossed
Broken or stoned
Right from the bottom
In tandem with your soul
Then where else
Should it be

Surely, not bound up
Closed off
Somewhere in your chest

What a waste

The heart is meant
To be exposed
To be laid bare

It is not meant to be chained

The willingness at which
We allow our heart to be pierced
Is the measure of bravery
In ourselves

Open the floodgates
And let your heart beat
Let it bleed

This is how you live a life
Worthy of experience
It is the curse of being human
And the gift of all gifts

I wonder

I wonder if I really love this house
Or if I've convinced myself of its greatness
Because we are here now

I wonder if I should be getting out more
If isolating myself is ok
Probably not
But being out in the general public
Pulls at my soul

I wonder if this table is really sanitary
If any of this is
And I wonder at my perfectionism

I wonder if this is all worth it
Because all I really want
Is to get back to my novel
To be in the grips of my imagination
I wonder if I stay there too much
Too long, these days

I wonder at my overuse of commas

I wonder if I'm ever doing what's right
What's good
Or if I've grown selfish in my older age
I want what I want
I wonder if that's why
That song appeals to me

I wonder if the teacher in front of me
Can help, can inspire
Perhaps break something open in me

I wonder why in the pursuit of things
Do I approach with the goal
Of getting something out of it

I wonder how to balance the pull
Of my imagination
With the reality before me

And I know the answer
I know all of them

I wonder if I'll keep making
The same decisions
Or if I'll finally grow tired
Of my own shit

I wonder how much of a role
My hormones are playing in this bout
This train of thought
I wonder at my original thought
And I wonder why I question it all

This place is my sanctuary
My safe space

This is my home

The Symphony

An invite
And a tag along

I extended it
As though it were an afterthought
And we both know
I had hoped
You'd say yes

And we dressed in our best
Didn't we

We walked through
That cold February air
And I struggle to recall
If you offered your coat
But it doesn't matter
It felt as though you did

A symphony
Composed around love
And we weren't quite there
But knew we were standing
On a precipice of something
Pretty great
And different
Maybe, mostly
For me

That night

You kissed me
Under the Christmas tree
That didn't belong there
And when you found
Both my hands
Something bigger told me
Of our future plans

I stayed in bed
Most of next morning
Daydreaming it all away

I pictured us
In every scenario
And it all felt so good
And right

We've tried to recreate
That night
And in sixteen years
We've come so close
But never on the mark

There is magic
In the firsts
Meant to be savored

And I did
And I have

These are all of the things
I carry with me

Sunshine

I give such warmth
On your cold days

Have you ever asked yourself
Why they're all so cold

And when you call
At random hours
And I answer in trepidation
Unbeknownst to you

Don't you wonder
Why I never ask
How you're doing

I listen
And I wait
Not patiently
You probably wouldn't know that

I ruminate on all of the years
And I cannot place
Where all of the love is
Where I find it
In patchwork
Is laced with something
I still can't put my finger on

Somewhere along the way
I decided to stop shining

For you
And it killed me
But you wouldn't know that
I never told you

I cannot be your sunshine
When all you do
Is douse me with your rain

The Threshold

Is the pursuit of creativity
And passion
And expressing yourself the reward
Or the outcome of the chase

It's about doing what you do
Just to do it
I think

Have you not asked yourself
If you can breathe
Something of your essence
Into the lives of others
Without anyone ever really knowing
How you did it

And in this world of voyeurism
It is a wicked game
Of not staring or lingering too long

Either way
I grapple with why it all has to be public anyway

Don't you just want to do what you want to do

But we want it on fire
We want to be seen
To not go unnoticed
We want to leave a mark
To contribute to the vast space and time

Of creativity and life and all that it means
We want to really mean something
And know that in the end
None of it was wasted

Certainly, there's a place for the mundane
The monotonous day in and day out
Kind of stuff that when taken away is missed

It's a lonely kind of gray winter day
If you're not careful
A beautiful life can get swallowed whole
And all of the gifts taken with it

It's the saddest of any story ever told

What I mean to say is
There is this space of fear and vulnerability
A place that rests right on the edge
Where you can see it, hear it, taste it
The sweetness of your creative endeavors
Resting in the space you imagined

This holding space

Toes dangling, gripping, holding on
It's the pit in your stomach
The quickening of the heart
The right before
The almost there
The hovering above publish or send
The setting it aside for just one more day

The second guessing

It's the ego driven statements that say
No one will get you
They will laugh
They will think you're having a mid-life crisis
They will project their own insecurities

And I will tell you
It will not matter in the end

It is but one step
One press of a button
An opening of a door
And you will have arrived

Creativity is a safe space
Where you can rest
Knowing that the hard part is over

Open your heart
Show us what you've got
It will never be wasted on us

Whether soft or loud
Just say what you mean

The Foundation

I lay in a strange bed
Surrounded by books and decor
Very much within my own taste
And I stared up at the roof
A small window cracked the light through

And when I closed my eyes
A kaleidoscope of colors began to swirl
In Rainbows played
And I did not know I was weeping
Until I touched my face

What looked and felt like grace
Was quickly swept away
And a funhouse of torture and mockery
Ebbed in and out of focus

I said I didn't like this
And it only made it worse

I threw myself from the bed
And announced to you
That I couldn't stop fighting it
But you were battling your own guilt

And so I laid back down
Covered myself up
And faced the truth

The noise silenced and I saw her

Just a child
Her innocence and trepidation
Mixed into an ugly tincture
His face a blur
But we both knew that look anywhere

I laid still as she squirmed
Afraid and not understanding
But I understood that I could not save her
From what was happening

And I needed to see it all
To understand
The crux
The foundation of what was laid
So long ago
What was taken from her
From me
So a healing could begin

I cannot unsee
But I also cannot reclaim
What was stolen
A childhood and purity so divine

We move through this life
With the best of intentions
But we cannot avoid or detect
The wrongdoings of others
Their own hurt skimming yours

And if it doesn't destroy you

Then you can destroy it yourself
And rebuild
Brick by brick
Stone by stone
A foundation of your choosing

Modern Day Mother

There's often not enough time
In the day
It seems
In this busy season of life

Minding the children
So young still
Tending to my thoughts
The connections we must keep
To our partner, family, and friends
A community at large

And where is the time for self care
To sit and to breathe
To really feel the sun on my skin
Without the mind wandering
Amongst all of the errands
The to-do's
The maintaining
Keeping it all afloat

And even more so

To keep a job
To keep them happy, too

Where is the time

What is more important

What has this world
This country
This life, become
That we are expected
To do all of this
And we are expected to do it
With a smile

Have gratitude
It could be worse

Well, I haven't slept in ages
And my bones are tired
My body buzzes
From the constant movement
The incessant thinking
The millions of thoughts that go in and out

And my legs go unshaven
And those cobwebs in the corners
They beckon my attention
But the moment I walk away
I forget

They are the most forgiving
The most reliable
Never really going anywhere

And I could not be more grateful

Choices

I look back
On all of the times
I've betrayed myself

And I had no idea
Other than I felt empty
And wrong

And living a life
Full of joy and feeling content
Felt further from anything

I did not feel gratitude
Just the cards that were dealt
And there was always so much anger
But mostly grief
For what I knew was missing
And what was never given

I can't say
That I did not ask to be born
Because who really knows anyway

But I know this much to be true
There is no solid blue print
Or a man leading our fate
There are choices made
First, by others
Until placed in our hands
And we can only choose

What we know best to be true
But there will be people and things
That get in the way
The derailment of it all

My point is this
Choose wisely
When you can
And know that wisdom
Shifts and changes

Looking back with regret
Or disdain
Will not serve you
And if you can bear
All of the roads traveled
And the destination you've reached
And your heart is still pieced
Then there are still choices ahead
To be made
Yours alone
If you're so brave

I Notice

I notice the neutral tones of my home
The quiet, as my children lay in bed
The peace I so desperately crave at times
The hum of the traffic
Like ocean waves
Until a siren blares through the streets

I notice the plants I tend to
With real feeling
My attempt to pull nature inside
Because going out in this society
Does not always feel so good

I notice the cold that seeps into this old house
Into my bones
Maybe the lack of movement
I wonder
Or the small cracks in the foundation
Of this place

I notice the dim lighting in the evening
A far cry from the abundance of sunshine
We are graced with
From the all of these windows
I coveted from the start

I notice the tidiness I obsess over
Constantly moving
Picking up
Putting away

I notice my tea is gone
The dregs are like ice
And my water is running low

The nails on my fingers
Long and sharp
Do I even like them like this
Or am I trying to channel someone else

I notice my guilt for not attending to my children today
For sticking them in front of the television
For succumbing to the frustrations
Of being pulled from what I want to do
The responsibility of having to entertain
When I just want to
Be

I notice a rhythmic sound
And I cannot place it
It reminds me of the noises my dog made
As he slept
He's been gone now for fourteen months
And that feels impossible

I like the noise
Whatever it is
Maybe it's just the refrigerator humming
But it brings me comfort

Coven

This dance we do
As women
Up against
Or for
Each other

I know the value
Of my body
The sway of my energy
That can influence
An entire room

It cannot help
But be taken in
A morsel
For imagination
Whether I like it
Or not

I don't dress for men
That play their games
And want it all
Just for the fun of it

Meanwhile
We dance in the moonlight
And shift the tides

We can heal
And calm

With mere words
And stares
The ultimate creators

And we spit fire
Like rain
If we so choose

There is nothing
More formidable
Than a woman
In her power

The Muse

I asked creativity
What it desired of me
And it said

Just show up
Be willing to see the simplicity
Of the sun shining through the trees
To feel the many privileges of your life
And the gratitude
Just waiting to burst through

Be willing to make time
Out of your precious day
And all of your responsibilities
And obligations
To sit with me for a while
And let me course my way through

Treat me as your most precious visitor
Understand I will never become
The annoying house guest
Although I too
Will never call first
And I will show up unannounced

But I will not demand anything of you
I will only wish for you
To feel the rising tension
And build something of it

I will not go knocking on other doors
I found you for a reason
I am sure of it
Of all the muses in the world
Of all the conduits
I saw you
And I could not unsee

My desire of you is this
Your willingness
Nothing more, nothing less

Inner Workings

There is a cottage along the sea
A weeping willow
And a porch swing

A wooden gate at the entrance
To such wildflower dreams

There is room to twirl
To roam
To bask in the sun
A respite amongst the loud
And tired world

And every version of me
That felt and endured
All of the sorrow and loneliness
Has taken solace here

I tend to them like flowers
Pouring every morsel
Of love
And joy
And gratitude
Into their souls

And they dance and rejoice
Each time I return
A greeting more ecstatic than the last

Never once have I seen them

Enter the cottage
Always frolicking in the fields

Freedom
At long last

It is not a suggestion
But a way to live

The Journey

I'll tell you of the last ten years or so
Of an intentional suffering I bestowed upon myself

Who does such things

When the suffering hit its peak
Its aperture widening
I knelt
My eyes as wide as I could bear

Most times I snapped them shut
To the awful, ugly, rotten to the core
Truth of it all
Every single thing handed down to me
And I swore I'd never open them again

But still, I knelt
And I continued on to the valleys
And the treacherous landscapes
The dark night of the soul, they say

It's always darkest before dawn
Light cannot shine without burning first
They'll say it all
And how cliché and how true

But there will come a time
When you surely realize
The map of such things
They do not mean to lead you astray

The roads, they even out
And your eyes adjust to the new light
Come see, it says
See all of your hard work

It is all so different, this landscape
And if not for all of its grandeur
You could mistaken it for being the same

But this one is ruled by love
Each inhale a reminder
That there is an exhale that awaits you

This Reminds Me

This reminds me of any other
Existential crisis I've ever had
A constant questioning and analyzing
Of every thought
And every action
Am I doing enough

Am I enough

This reminds me of all the second-guessing
Of my childhood
With no guidance
No one to tell me what's what

This reminds me
That it doesn't matter
Not really
We are who we are
And it'll be what it'll be

This reminds me of her sometimes
I feel her in me
And it doesn't feel the best
This reminds me that she didn't have any goodness
In her back then, anyway

This reminds me of what still remains
And what can flair
If left unchecked
This reminds me that we are forever learning

This reminds me of acceptance
And grace
And gratitude

This reminds me of my heart
And why I'm here, now
Not any other time frame
Not then
Not if

This reminds me of my choices
Moment by moment
And what I choose going forward
What I have chosen
And what's gotten me here

This reminds me of what's important
What I've brought into this space

This reminds me of compassion
For myself, mostly
Because if it's vacant here
It's certainly not over there

Worst Version

We're all really
Just one short circuit away
From becoming the worst version
Of ourselves

And I'm within another version
That doesn't feel like carrying the weight
Today
Or any other day

There's a mixture of sadness and laziness
And the other is screaming out
Muffled
And completely ignored

Can we blame the hormones
The changing of my body
The circumstances of my life
And past conditioning
The rain that's falling from the sky, maybe
Or the disconnect with people
The inflation and defeat
The movie that made me sad
And reminded me too much of my ex

I'll wake up tomorrow
And it'll be sunny
And my disposition
Back on its feet

I'll laugh at the drama
Tell her to chill with it all
But really, she's just firing up
Waiting to turn it on
When there's a valid reason

And I cannot blame her
When we're in the dead of winter
And the only months ahead
Are the coldest of the season

This is 40

Abandoning myself
In every version
Became a closed book
In middle age

The toddler
Forced to see and feel
Such scary things

The school age girl
Wrecked by deceitful friends
A shameful environment
Guided by abuse and abandonment

The middle schooler
Running so far from it all
Trying to fill her own cup
Not even knowing
It was filled with holes

The teenager
Searching out love
In all of the wrong places

The young woman
Roaming
Not of freedom
But ties being cut

The mother

So determined and headstrong
Not to fuck it all up
Pushing and pushing and pushing through
Gathering such tools
She had no idea how to use

And we all met
At this middle aged place of wonder
And acceptance
And love
And breakthroughs
With all of our faults
And hardships
And lessons learned

And we burned it all down
To start anew

What remained were the tools
With sudden purpose
And determination

I found me
For now
The accumulation of all things past
The hopes and desires of the future
But mostly the now
The messy
The hopeful
The joy of it all

Nap Time

Each time you say
Please lay with me
And I choose not to
I feel the future mourning

I am much too busy
There are things to do
Laundry to be folded
Dishes to be done
My mind to quiet
If only for my own sake

I watch your small body
Your chest rise and fall
Rise and fall

And my heart aches to be with you
But my mind says there is much to be done

But to lie beside you
To feel your sweet breath on my cheek
Your hair tousled with sweat

You'll wake in an hour or so
And you'll call for me
And I'll breathe you in
And I'll say to myself
Next time
Next time I'll lay down

And oh, do I know the agony
That there will come a day
That there will be no next time

It comes without warning
And you won't realize it
Until much later
That the opportunity
That cute thing they always did
Always asked you for
Always said

It is gone

And how long has it been now
We struggle to remember

Isn't that the crux of it all
The pure joy of watching a life grow
The pure agony of watching a life grow

Christmas 2024

I'll want to remember this
A Christmas Eve
Waking in your seventh year
And your fourth

We opened the blinds
To fresh snow falling
And I said
How perfect is this

We've got the day
To do whatever we please
Nowhere to go
Unimportant things to do

Our home is so warm
And there is an abundance
Everywhere you look
Every gift under the tree
Just extra

We have everything we need
Everything we could ever want
Right at our fingertips

Today I'll paint your nails
In shades of red and green
You'll play in the snow
And I'll wait inside
Warming the hot chocolate

I don't know
How it all came to be
All of these ideas
And the love flowing
So freely
The ideal picture
Painted so easily

I used to wonder
Why I had been given
A life so agonized
And then I grew
To make something different
For myself

Complete with the three of you
And so much more
Than I ever could have imagined

The Trickster

What if I told you
I took this part
For myself

Manipulated
All of the scenarios
To bend to my will

And I've practiced
Contorting my face
And my expressions
To match what you'd like
To see

I can weave my words
Leading you
Right where I want you
To go

And I'll bide my time
If it means
You believe it was your own choice

My patience
Far outweighs my innocence

And isn't this who I am
Who I was bred to be
This cunning woman
Wielding such power

Am I to blame
If you're too blind
To see

Isn't that what they say
All parts exist
But we deny most

I haven't exiled this one
So much as she's hidden
Behind a veil
And I guess they're right
About us
We're one long line
Of witches
Knowing damn well
What we do

And if it angers you
Tell me
What hides behind your veil

What parts of you ache
To see the light of day

Winter

There is such dampness
And cold
That permeates the bones
On days like these

The rain is freezing
And we stay huddled in
Cutting off from connection
As a means of comfort
And survival

I awoke from a dream
Of you
The water was murky
And I could not place
Where we were

Your head under
And you sank further and further
The harder I swam
I could not reach you
Until you became
A part of it

I came up for air
But I could never really breathe
After that

You were gone
And my chest forgot how to rise

It couldn't remember how to intake
Anything, much less air

I spent the morning
Wrapping myself tighter and tighter
Against the cold
And the dread of my thoughts

I held you as tightly
As I could manage
Without you squirming for freedom

There's nothing more unsettling
Than the weather matching your mood
And your thoughts

There is no reprieve
And these days seem so long
And unforgiving
I fear my mind is settling
With the grey
And the cold
Washing itself of any warmth

And what hope is there
When it intercedes
With my dreams
A place I counted on
As safe and right

Joy

I used to hurry through life
Always somewhere to be
Someone to see
Things to do
A pre-teen wanting to be sixteen
And sixteen served up depression and confusion

When my children were babies
I said I couldn't wait
Until they sleep through the night
Now I watch them sleep

I couldn't wait until
There were no more diapers to change
And I miss the intimacy of those moments

I couldn't wait to turn thirty
To leave the peril of my twenties
But oh, did they bring
Such work and inner turmoil

And so I took everything from my thirties
And brought it with me to forty
Alchemized into something more useful
And less heavy

I sat with my fine lines
And my changed body
And I breathed my children in

I felt everything there was to feel
And I did not run
For once in my life

I walked through boredom
And ebbed with the flowing
Of three year old tantrums

And when I laughed
I really felt the constriction
Of my belly
And the joy it turned into
I do not wait
I do not want
Or wish

What a joy it is to be this living thing

A Delusion of Sorts

I have set apart
What's real
And what's in front of me
For the many lives
We have lived in my mind

I hop back and forth
A master of illusion
Disconnecting
Even from the road I'm driving
And I will end up
Somewhere
I have no remembrance
Of traveling to

But there we were
As clear as day
You played me your favorites
And I fed you mine
We danced in the grass
Overlooking the woods
And you sang to me
All of your songs

I built our life
In a thirty minute commute
And you said
You were never happier

I click in and out

To and fro
And the only winner here
Is me
Leaving you stand alone
In the confines of my mind

Such a dirty trick I play
On my own heart
When all I'm really winning at
Is the loss of time
And connection
To what's right here
In front of me

Easter Morning

We were back in that apartment
The attic I shared
With my sisters
Where no good memories
Can be recalled

And I awoke to the noises
My fantasy-rich mind cultivated
Telling me to go
Hurry up
There is magic
Just down the stairs

I chased that rabbit
And I swear
I could see him so clear

But he was gone
And in his place
Hushed arguments ensued
And when my presence
Became known
It escalated so rapidly

Playing tug of war
With my body

Any love
And panic
For my well being

Was smothered
By the need to be right
And to have the last word

A pawn
In such a dangerous game

I awoke
With the sun
And the excitement
Of the day
And I felt the fog
And haze of it all
Like a dream
Within a dream

But I knew
I had chased that rabbit
And I knew
In the deepest part of my soul
That it was as real
As the marks
Left on my body

Halcyon

The seasons changed
And I let go
But not of my own volition

The cold swept through
And shook me
In all its austerity

I smirked
At all of its likeness

It's something, isn't it

Much like the bare trees
I have been stripped down
To nothingness
Unrecognizable to myself

Any accompaniments
Left hanging on
By a thread
Bear no semblance

And it's just as well

They'll shake loose
Like the others

I would have buckled
In my youth

To be rattled so hard
Parading my martyrdom
To bent ears
My hands filled
With such torment

To live in such a way

And to find myself here
Charming the wind and the waves

The twenty second of days
Such a gift
A loss of composure
Surely bound to right itself

Spring will rise again
I'm sure of it

The Reveal

If I cannot sail or fly
Perhaps ride my way
To the life and the experiences
That surely must claim more excitement than this
Then I will stay

I'll conjure the warmth of a sunny day
And marvel at the singing birds
Still perched on the neighbor's roof
In the middle of November

I will move my feet
Swing in the hammock
The blue cloudy sky
A pendulum of wonder

(And the laughter of my children)

The random roar of any given moment
Just waiting to be revealed
Isn't that the work in and of itself
To find the beauty in the mundane
To land and ground right where you are

For heaven's sake
This isn't a respite
This is your life
You better start living it

When It's Good

What's better in this life
Than this

The echoes of joy
Found in every square inch
Of a life, a home, a family
You've created for yourself

The memory of a photograph
A dent in the floor
From the matchbox cars
Thrown haphazardly in toddlerhood
A forgotten art project on the table
Another sequin stuck
To the bottom of your shoe

It changes
And it disappears

Presence is not a choice
But a must

The secret to life
Is knowing it's good
When it's good

Ever Changing

I understand the need to check out
Don't you

When the chaos is so deafening
And the exhaustions hit their peak
It's been running and running
And taking and waiting
Serving and helping
And nodding
And smiles and breath work
When it's just not about you
Anymore

I understand that

The body and the mind
Ever-changing
Forced and pushed
To grow
To meet it all
Where it's at

Don't you get lost
In the shuffle
A shell of a former self
But all for the better

And my heart
Has grown outside of me
Twice over

There's such wonder and love there too

And that's the curse of it all
The beauty and light
Mixed in such ugliness and dark
A pendulum
Of highs and lows
Joy and utter desperation

I understand the need to check out
It could just swallow you whole

A Vulgar Display of Love

I've become everything
We needed when we were young

In such a dark uncertainty
I became what's sure
And light
In this world

A self imposed excavation
Of all that lay dormant
And I exposed it all to myself

I re-watched the abuse
From dirty hands
And leather belts
As they stripped away
And beat the joy out of me
Igniting fear and mistrust

What a vulgar display of love
You were

I ran with it for years
Allowing sadness
And half-hearted apologies
From men and bosses
And magazines and peers
To dominate my world
And convince me even further
That I was somehow

Not enough

The price I have paid
For such makeshift guidance

And so I ran from it for years
Until I found myself
Mothering my own

And I watched the soft miracle
Of their lives
Shape and form my heart back
To something recognizable
A distant whisper
Turned to a loud roar
That I could not turn from anymore

I cannot imagine
Breaking their hearts

My unearthing of self
Has had no limits
To elation and delight
Despite the constant willingness
To break myself
Over and over again

And in my recompense
I get to live freely
Unbound by such carelessness

And yet I hope

You're not left in your vulgarity

That someway, somehow
You have found a way
Back to love
And all that it means

Persistence

I have stayed
Despite it all
I have endured
I have faced myself
Time and again
And all I have come away with
Is my stubborn persistence
To love and be loved

Sheena Stimpfl is the writer of several novels, as well as her Substack, *Buckle Up, I'm Weird Now*, where you can find her non-fiction writing in essay form. When she's not writing, she's a copyeditor, proofreader, and sometimes photographer. Sheena lives in the Lehigh Valley, Pennsylvania with her husband and two children.

www.ingramcontent.com/pod-product-compliance
Lightning Source LLC
Chambersburg PA
CBHW010939120626
46554CB00008B/2540